D is for DOGGO!

The Most Heckin' Good Book of DOGGOLINGO

Kelly Kandra Hughes

Kelly Kandra Hughes, Ph.D., loves dogs. Even though her Ph.D. is in psychology, she thinks it's hilarious to tell people her Ph.D. stands for "professional house and dog sitter." Kelly travels across the country with her husband to provide the best possible care for people's homes and furry family members while the humans arc away. They have so far worked in Alberta, Colorado, Connecticut, Illinois, Massachusetts, New York, North Carolina, Tennessee, and Washington.

Photos commercially licensed from Shutterstock and Dreamstime, except:
Copyright Page Bulldog: *rawpixel.com;* "So What Do You Say" King Cavalier Charles, French Bulldog, White Terrier, Daschund: *Master1305* at Freepik.com

Hardback: 979-8-9892421-0-8
Softcover: 979-8-9892421-1-5

Cover & Book Design by Joni Nemeth www.joninemeth.com

Frisky Dog Press
PO Box 300
Norfolk, CT 06058

To all the

GOOD and

HECKIN' GOOD

dogs everywhere!

So, really, all dogs ever.

A is for AROO!

AROOs are for dogs
who have lots to say.
Bossing their human,
'til they get their way.
Or sometimes **AROO**s
are simply for joy,
sung round and around
for *"good girl or boy!"*

B is for BOOP

BOOPs are for kisses
or taps on the nose.
Just keep in mind—
not *anything goes.*
BOOPs should be gentle
and also quite sweet.
BOOPs should be loving,
the best kind of treat.

C is for CLOUD

CLOUDs are white doggos that fell from the sky,
soft like a pillow and sweet like a pie.
Some **CLOUD**s are giant and some **CLOUD**s are not,
but each **CLOUD** is loved for all that they've got!

D is for DOGGO

DOGGOs are perfect
in so many ways!
That's why we love them,
for all of our days.
Loyal and happy,
just look at that grin—
best friends forever,
through thick
and through thin.

E is for ERP!

Wow, what an **ERP!**
  That happened so fast.
That look on their face,
  it never does last.
ERPs come from surprise
  or moments of doubt.
But doggos are smart,
  they *will* **ERP** it out.

F is for FLOOF

A **FLOOF** is a dog with
mountains of fluff;
oodles and oodles,
yes, one giant puff.
FLOOFs can be sneaky;
they may not play fair.
One hug from a **FLOOF**—
you're covered
in hair!

G is for GOOD

GOOD is a word
that dogs love to hear.
Just say it once
and watch how they cheer.
Tails start waggin',
quick as a snap.
And if you're lucky,
paws tippy tap!

H is for HECKIN' GOOD

HECKIN' GOOD dogs
have got lots of flair!
So really, all dogs,
we're *not* talking rare.
No matter the dog,
no matter the place,
look in their eyes—
HECKIN' GOOD
is the case!

I is for ICKLES

ICKLES are teeny, they're tiny like tots.
No matter their size,
they have BIG DOG thoughts!
ICKLES have gumption, tenacity too.
Don't judge by their size,
what **ICKLES** can do.

J is for JIFFLE!

JIFFLEs are wiggles and waggles of fun!
Dogs love to **JIFFLE**
come rain or come sun.
They'll roll all around, with paws in the air—
footloose and happy
with nary a care.

K is for KIPPER

KIPPERs take snoozles all hours of day.
They sleep like a champ, except when they play.
Dozing and napping and siestas, too—
all are for **KIPPER**s, 'cuz that's what they do.

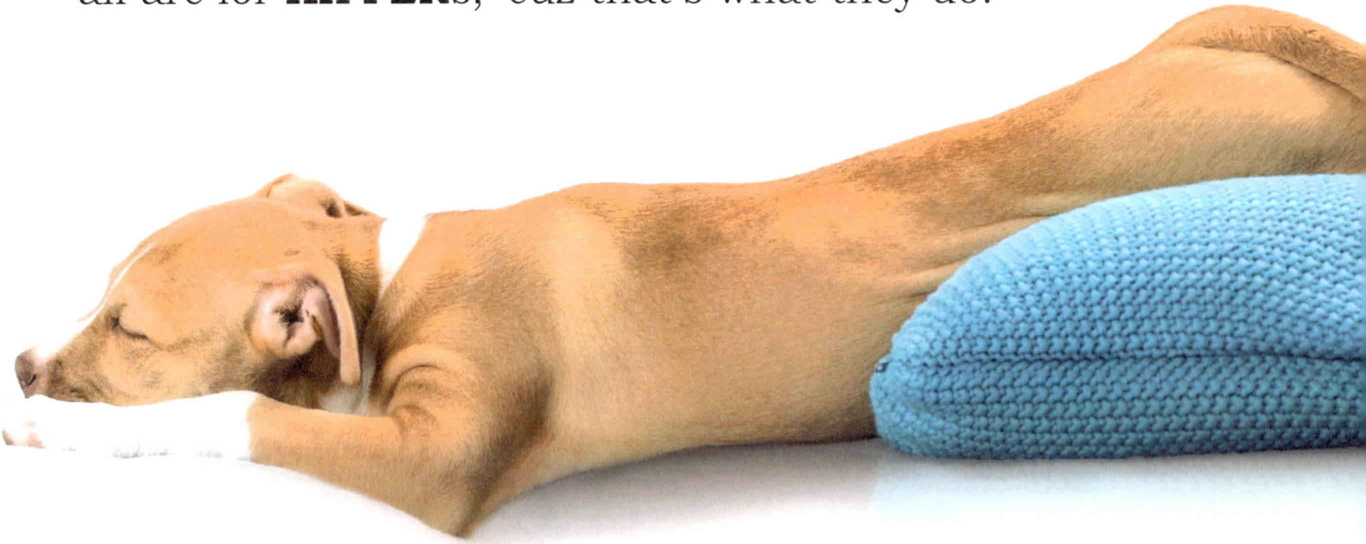

L is for LOAF

Look at that **LOAF**!
So pudgy and round,
with squat little legs
not high off the ground.
Roly and poly
and really quite cute;
Fetching and winsome
and charming to boot.

M is for

MLEP!

A **MLEP** happens fast,
a slip of the tongue.
No matter the age,
from old pups to young.
Some **MLEP**s you'll see
and some **MLEP**s you'll miss.
But get close enough,
you **MLEP** get a kiss!

N is for NUGGET

NUGGETs are precious,
we can't get enough.
Bite sized and perfect,
a nubbins of fluff.
We chew on their ears
and eat them all up—
(Not really, of course,
'cuz they're still a pup!)

Watch out for **OOMPA**s—
a rare breed of clown!
They jiffle and prance.
They *may* knock you down.
Jolly and happy,
a heckin' good friend.
OOMPAs are awesome,
no need to pretend.

O is for OOMPA

Then there are **PUPPER**s,
first-class at their game!
For looking so cute—
it's all in their name.
We ooh and we ahh,
can't help carry on;
PUPPERs are perfect,
pure dog paragon.

P is for PUPPER

Q is for QUEEN

A **QUEEN** is a dog who's sassy and posh;
they enter a room and people say, *"Gosh!*
Look at that doggo – have you ever seen
such polish and poise, they must be a ***QUEEN!"***

R is for RUMP

Some dogs have booties
best known as a **RUMP**.
They shake back and forth,
a perfect round lump.
Just watch them keep time,
it's truly a feat—
for **RUMP**s are spot on,
for keeping a beat.

S is for SAUSAGE

A **SAUSAGE** enchants
-- you'll be mesmerized!
Same as a nugget,
but more super-sized.
Burly and beefy,
a fine lump of meat—
some may be spicy
and some
may be sweet.

T is for TIPPY TAP

TIPPY TAP paws
dance and delight,
stampin' around
from mornin' to night.
Clickety clack!
Over the floor—
TIPPY TAP paws—
you know we adore.

U is for UNICORN

A **UNICORN** dog will up and appear
every so often, perhaps once a year.
Get out your streamers; invite all your mates—
a heckin' good time most certainly waits!

No pup is perfect,

oh wait. That's not true.

All pups are perfect,

oh yes. That we knew.

It's why every pup has **VIP** cred

Very Important.

Yep!

Just what we said.

V is for VIP

W is for WOOFER

WOOFERs are doggos who bark a good game.
Telling their tales or asking your name.
Woofing and barking to share all their news,
WOOFERs keep going,

except when
they snooze.

X is for XEEBLES

When meeting a **XEEBLES**,
you may have the thought:
Maximum sausage!
Oh, yes—they're a lot.
OVER-SIZED,
CHUNKY,
GRANDE,
XL—
the thing about **XEEBLES**,
they wear it so well.

Y is for YAPPER

YAPPERs are woofers,
just mini-me size
Hittin' the high notes—
oh, hear their cries!
Howlin' and growlin'
and maybe aroos,
yappin' around,
singing their blues.

ZOOMIES are something
you really should see
Zigging and zagging
and running so free
Fast as a cheetah.
No, wait—that's a cat!
Fast as a greyhound—
now *we'll* zoom to that.

Z is for ZOOMIES!

Oh no,
that's the end,
we've gone

A to Z.

We hope you enjoyed
our alphabet spree.
You have all the words;
it's now time to play.

The doggos are ready!

SO...

WHAT DO YOU SAY?

Printed in the USA
CPSIA information can be obtained
at www.ICGtesting.com
LVRC091527180124
769072LV00066B/210

* 9 7 9 8 9 8 9 2 4 2 1 1 5 *